MAXIMIZE YOUR TAX DEDUCTIONS

MICHAEL J. HOVELL, EA

MAXIMIZE YOUR TAX DEDUCTIONS

FOR BUSINESS OWNERS
GIG WORKERS
AND SIDE
HUSTLERS

MICHAEL J. HOVELL, EA

EAMIKE.COM

DEDICATION

MALEESA MOONEY
1991 - 2023

In the memory of my friend Maleesa Mooney. We only knew eachother for a short time, but your love for life, unlimited kindness and generosity made a profound impact on me and everyone you knew. You would have been a top Miami real estate agent, a successful entrepreneur and an inspiration to many. I miss you Maleesa.

Thank you to:

VITA Volunteer Income Tax Assistance;

Robert Clovey CPA, Michael Goldfine CPA, Gary Testa CPA;

Beverly Hovell, Frank Rizzuto, Aysel Mansley, and Mishal Khalid.

LEGAL DISCLAIMER

This book is the professional opinion of the author and is for informational purposes. It does not contain legal advice nor does it make any legal guarantees and should not be cited as legal authority. It is the reader's responsibility to conduct their own due diligence, as well as consult with tax professionals knowledgeable in the matters discussed herein. Please do not deal with the IRS without experienced representation.

Source of Law

The Tax Code, IRC or Internal Revenue Code is found in Title 26 of the United States Code, abbreviated 26 USC. The IRS issues publications providing guidance on all aspects of tax law, however while these publications explain tax law, they are not law, and can not be relied upon in court as a source of law.

IRS Publications

On the Works Cited page at the back of the book is a listing of the IRS Publications relevant to the topics in this book. There is citing used throughout this book based on the IRS Publications.

In-Text Citations

(463, p 8) is a citation used in Chapter 11, which means IRS Publication 463, page 8.

Message to Entrepreneurs

Dear Business Owners, Gig Workers and Side Hustlers,

As the amount of self-employed taxpayers increases, it has become more difficult for the government to track all of these transactions and collect all of the taxes they believe are owed. They have changed the laws in order to track and tax more of that money. With these new reporting requirements for payment platforms like Cashapp, Venmo, Paypal and others, self-employed taxpayers will have more of their income reported to the IRS than ever before. This means it is crucial for all of you Side Hustlers and Gig Workers to prepare for these changes, in order to keep more of your money.

In 2021, the US Congress reduced the filing threshold of Form 1099-K for payment platforms from $20,000 to $600. This was due to take effect for the 2022 tax year but was postponed when it became clear the difficulties this was going to cause. On November 21, 2023 the IRS again has delayed the new reporting requirements and even though the law still stands it will not be in effect for the 2023 tax year.

Income reporting using the Form 1099-K is flawed. The Form 1099-NEC already reports money paid to self-employed taxpayers from the customers, employers or other source of funds. Payment providers are just a conduit for the money transfers and requiring them to report as well, can lead to the double reporting of income. The IRS has no way of reconciling these two reporting methods to account for the double reporting error. I have already seen instances of over reporting of income from the Form 1099-K and have helped clients prove the reporting error to the IRS.

Also passed in 2021 by congress, is the Corporate Transparency Act (CTA), also set to begin January 1, 2024. The CTA mandates extra disclosure from owners of business entities. It is important to keep accurate books and records, store receipts and register a business entity. As a gig worker, side hustler, contractor or consultant, you are self-employed and the IRS treats you as a business owner. Your best course of action is to act like a business owner to take advantage of your self-employed tax status.

You need to register your businesses correctly to keep from overpaying on taxes. Read on to learn how to properly deduct car expenses, personal and business travel, a home office, fringe benefits like health and childcare and more. Also, learn how to structure your businesses to maximize tax deductions, avoid paying the extra tax on self-employment income and even how to correctly employ your children and spouse for even more tax savings.

Michael J. Hovell, EA

CONTENTS

CONTENTS

PREFACE

"In America, there are two tax systems, one for the informed and one for the uninformed. Both systems are legal." -- Judge Learned Hand

The tax system is one of the most important, but least understood systems in America. Deliberately confusing and overly complex, most taxpayers have no choice but to take their accountant's word. Every attempt to simplify the code has failed because every deduction has a constituency. Americans love the tax deductions they get, while hating the tax deductions other people get.

When students ask me, "Isn't income tax illegal?" I reply, "legal or illegal, try not paying income tax and see what happens." On that note, this is not a tax protest book, nor will I argue against the tax code's legitimacy, regardless of my personal opinion. This book teaches you how to use the tax code, as it is written, to your advantage. Just as Judge Hand said, being informed when it comes to tax law is as if there is a different tax code just for you. This is why tax law is written to confuse people.

The US Constitution authorizes the US Congress to impose and collect taxes, and they delegate tax administration to the IRS. The IRS does not create tax law, only congress can do that. The IRS does however, issue rulings, procedures, letters, and memoranda it believes to be inline with their mandate. They aren't always right. Taxpayers can challenge the IRS through different procedures within the IRS, consult the IRS internal Taxpayer Advocate or even petition the US Tax Court to hear their case. That being said, taxpayers should think twice about dealing with the IRS without proper representation.

As I have already mentioned in my "Message to Entrepreneurs," the recent changes in the law, many self-employed taxpayers and those engaged in side businesses, are about to get slammed with taxes and fees they haven't had to pay before. Just registering a business correctly can make a huge difference in the amount of taxes owed. When opening and operating a business, there are legal, accounting and tax related matters that need to be considered and many only find out what they should have known when it is already too late.

This book is delivered in two main sections: business and tax. Part I explains the different business entities available and how to form them. Part II explains how to use those business entities with the tax laws to maximize tax savings. Before we dive in, here are some answers to frequently asked questions relevant to the scope of this book.

FAQ

What is a business?

An activity engaged in with the intent of making a profit. When getting paid as a non-employee, reported on a 1099-NEC, you are considered to be in business as a Self- Employed Contractor or Sole Proprietor.

What is a business entity?

A formal legal creation that separates the business from the owners. Legally forming the entity "births" a fictitious person sometimes called Corporate Personhood. This separate being can sue and be sued, can contract in its own name and has constitutional rights.

Does business need a profit?

Businesses without a formal legal entity are not separate from the owners, making the taxpayer a sole proprietor or self-employed contractor. Self-employed taxpayers need to earn profits 3 out of 5 years, or the IRS can reclassify the business as a hobby. However, corporations can lose money every year as long as they have the intent to make a profit. Legally organizing and registering a business can be evidence of one's profit intent.

What is a dba?

DBA stands for Doing Business As and is used when conducting business under a different name, known as a trade name, assumed name or fictitious name. Since a sole-proprietor doesn't have a legal entity registered, they would register a dba to attach the business name to their name, like John Doe dba John's Pizza. Corporations may choose to use a dba for a brand name without opening a new entity for the brand itself.

Business owners, buy assets in personal name or business?

We have a very litigious society, and anyone owning assets and earning income in their own name can become targets as lawyers are on the lookout for what they call "deep pocket defendants." You want to have business entities between you and your assets, such as the Limited Liability Company, Limited Partnership, Land Trust, etc. Placing business or other legal entities between the person and their assets provides asset protection as well as tax reduction benefits. However, there can be complications when financing your assets through a bank and one may need to seek alternative lenders, which also needs to be considered when making this decision. It is also very important to be familar with and knowledgeable in the state and local real estate laws.

Why do businesses get special tax treatment?

There is a saying, "The business of America is business." The economy as a whole, and the job market in particular, require wealthy people and businesses to put their money to work. To encourage investment and job creation, the US government finds it advantageous to pass laws incentivizing entrepreneurship, business ownership, investing, real estate development, and other activities that benefit society as a whole.

There is a fundamental misunderstanding about money, wealth, business and economics in this country built off of resentment. When the mood of America turns anti-business, businesses just move their operations to other countries for cheaper labor, lower taxes and better laws. Is that punishing the business owner or the American worker?

What is a tax shelter?

A Tax Shelter is an activity, asset or investment that shields income, offering "shelter" from being taxed. It's like giving an umbrella to your income to shelter it from the storm that is the IRS. The government, in attempting to encourage or discourage behavior or investment, offers different tax treatment to different activities. Taxpayers pay tax on taxable income, not their gross income. This allows taxpayers to report income in their gross income that does not count in their taxable income, thereby sheltering that income from being taxed.

Aren't tax shelters illegal?

It depends on the type of tax shelter. There used to be more tax shelters available offering better benefits than most of the tax shelters of today. Many of the more well-known and popular tax shelters were specifically targeted and yes, are now illegal. So, to answer the question, illegal tax shelters are illegal. Not only are they illegal to do, they are illegal to promote as well. Once a tax shelter is classified as "abusive" it becomes illegal to promote that tax shelter to clients and customers. Tax law is a constantly evolving system that requires constant attention. (550, p 26)

What is the difference between tax evasion and tax avoidance?

Legality - The most obvious difference is Tax Avoidance is legal and Tax Evasion is illegal. There are ambiguities in the tax law, and different people have different interpretations, sometimes referred to as a "gray area." The US Tax Court does rule against the IRS showing that tax law isn't as black and white as the IRS would like people to believe, but usually has a touch of gray.

Intent - In an audit, a sincere and good faith argument must be made to back up the different interpretations. Even if you don't win on the merits, it can help in abating penalties, and make a record there was no criminal intent, just a misunderstanding.

Motive - Taxpayers can't engage in activities for the sole purpose of tax reduction. However, there's nothing wrong with engaging in activities for other reasons that just so happen to result in tax reduction. Taxpayers should be prepared to argue the non-tax related reasons for a tax avoidance transaction.

Disclosure - Taxpayers have reporting requirements that go beyond income and expenses, specifically when it comes to foreign assets and accounts, as well as certain cryptocurrency transactions, among others.

Under Reporting - Willfully not reporting reportable income is Tax Evasion and illegal. Reporting income in a way in which it can't be taxed, taxed at a lower rate, or taxed in a later year, is Tax Avoidance and legal when done correctly and for the right reasons.

PART I

BUSINESS AND ENTITIES

CHAPTER ONE

INTRODUCTION TO ENTITIES

E ntity theory is the idea that a business is separate from its owners. For legal and accounting purposes the business is a person that has rights, can sue and be sued, can contract in its own name and is an artificial, but legal person.

The following two chapters are a general overview of the main entity types one can choose when organizing a business. They are listed from simplest and cheapest to open and maintain to the most complex and expensive. The entities covered here, in order of complexity, are sole proprietorship, partnership, Limited Liability Company, S-Corporation and C-Corporation.

There are also sub-entity types such as limited partnerships, single member and multi-member LLC, professional LLC and more.

In Appendix E at the end of the book, there is a chart comparing the general details of the main entity types. One must remember that in the US, entities are formed at the state level, and while most states are generally similar, differences need to be recognized and accounted for.

There are also additional entities beyond the scope of this book, such as Non-Profits like Foundations and Charities and special purpose entities such as Trusts and Estates. These entities can be incredibly complex; consult experienced professionals that specialize in those areas.

Chapter Two

Unincorporated Entities

According to IRS statistics, the vast majority of businesses (80%) in the United States, filing a tax return, are unincorporated. 70% are Sole Proprietorships, with no formal legal structure. General partnerships also have no official registration requirements, in most cases.

Owners of unincorporated businesses pay their business taxes on their personal tax return. They can usually recognize business losses to reduce their taxable income.

Unincorporated business owners are not employees of their company and do not earn wages. They will have to pay an additional 15% tax on profits called Self-Employment Tax. This extra tax replaces payroll taxes usually paid on employee wages.

Sole Proprietorship

This is not an actual entity, and is not separate from the owner. Only one owner is allowed, though there is an exception for married couples (see Qualified Joint Venture, below). Ownership cannot be transferred or sold. Since the business and the owner are not separate, business activity, income, expenses, and taxes are filed and paid on the personal income tax return of the owner, Form 1040, Schedule C. This structure leaves the owner fully liable for the debts of the business, but this issue can be somewhat mitigated with a good business insurance policy.

Qualified Joint Venture - Married couples running an unincorporated business, have the option of making a voluntary election for a qualified joint venture instead of a partnership. All income and expenses of the sole proprietorship are split in half as a joint venture. In this case, two identical Schedule C forms are attached to the 1040 if filing a joint tax return.

Partnerships

General Partnership The simplest form of partnership, consisting of two or more owners, which is similar to the spousal joint venture above. All partners of a general partnership are fully liable for debts and obligations of the partnership and pay taxes on their share of the profits whether or not they receive the money. A partnership is a "pass-through entity" in that its taxable income is computed on its own return, Form 1065, and passed through a Schedule K-1 to the personal returns of the partners, on Form 1040, Schedule E.

Limited Partnership (LP) Formed with the state and consisting of one or more general partners with unlimited liability and one or more limited partners who gain liability protection as long as their role in the business is also limited. Limited partners cannot be involved in management decisions and should remain silent partners to protect their limited liability.

Limited Liability Partnership (LLP) Usually very similar to a general partnership in unlimited liability for regular company debts, but there are protections for partners from the liabilities and lawsuits brought against the other partners for negligence and other alleged misbehavior.

Limited Liability Limited Partnership (LLLP) A new entity available in about 30 out of 50 states, as of August 2022. It's a hybrid of the LP and LLP where partners have liability protection from the regular debts of the partnership and from liabilities of the other partners.

Family Limited Partnership (FLP) An entity usually used in estate planning to achieve inter-generational wealth preservation for wealthy families. Assets would be held jointly by family members with special provisions written into the partnership agreement. Earnings generated by the partnership would be paid to family members as dividends.

Limited Liability Company, LLC

LLCs have "members" instead of owners or shareholders, and can choose to be managed by a member or an outside manager. It's a popular entity to form since it offers the liability protections of corporations, without the maintenance costs and filing requirements of corporations. The LLC also offers flexibility in choosing how it wants to be taxed.

Single Member LLC, sometimes written SMLLC, is made up of one member and by default is considered a non-entity for tax purposes. The registered legal entity is disregarded, taxing the member as if they were a sole proprietor. However, by filing Form 8832, it can choose to be treated as a corporation for tax purposes.

Multi Member LLC is made up of more than one member and by default is treated as a partnership for tax purposes. Like the SMLLC, an MMLLC or just LLC, can also elect to be taxed as a corporation by filing Form 8832.

Professional LLC, written as PLLC, is a business entity designed for licensed professionals, such as lawyers, doctors, architects, engineers, accountants, and chiropractors. Some states don't allow LLCs to be owned by licensed professionals and those who want the benefits of an LLC must form a PLLC instead. Depending on the profession and the state, members will need approval from their state licensing board during the formation process. Most states only allow licensed professionals to be members in a PLLC.

Series LLC - written as SLLC, is a new type of LLC which can be formed in 23 out of 50 states, as of the writing of this book, August 2022. The purpose of the SLLC is to achieve the outcome of owning multiple LLCs but in a less complex and more affordable way. Even in the states that offer the SLLC, there are significant differences in forming and maintaining the separate series or cells, within a series LLC. In addition, it is not yet clear to what degree states without Series LLC laws will honor a Series LLC formed in another state.

Chapter Three

Incorporated Entities

There are legal formalities that are supposed to be followed when incorporating. Much of it is window dressing and paper signing for small and micro businesses, but can have severe legal consequences for medium and large businesses. An Incorporator is responsible for the initial filings with the state for the Articles of Incorporation. The Incorporator holds a meeting for shareholders at which directors are elected, and whoever becomes the Chairman of the Board of Directors takes over the meeting from the Incorporator. Minutes are kept, the bylaws are read and adopted, resolutions are passed, and Corporate Officers may be appointed.

C-Corporation

This is the only entity that pays its own income taxes on a business tax return. The corporation pays tax on its profits on Form 1120, and any dividends distributed to shareholders will be taxed again on the shareholders' personal returns, resulting in double taxation.

To minimize the negative effects of double taxation, C-Corps are able to deduct expenses not afforded to other entity types. The expenses usually take the form of fringe benefits offered to employees such as retirement accounts, health coverage, expense reimbursement plans, among others. These benefits can be given to employees tax free or tax preferred, but require proper planning and documentation.

When a C-Corporation has a loss in a particular year, it is referred to as a Net Operating Loss, NOL for short. While this net operating loss can no longer be carried backward to receive a refund on prior years taxes, it can still be carried forward to reduce future tax liabilities.

S-Corporation

Another way to mitigate double taxation is for the C-Corporation to file a Form 2553, Election by a Small Business Corporation. This election is requesting the IRS tax the corporation as a pass-through entity which transitions the C-Corporation into an S-Corporation.

After receiving approval from the IRS, the state needs to be notified. Any and All shareholders in a given year, have to agree for the S Election to be approved. Other requirements are the Corporation must be domestic, with no business shareholders or foreign shareholders, and there can't be more than 100 shareholders.

In addition to offering protection from double taxation of profits, the S-Corp limits the exposure to self-employment taxes charged to the owners of unincorporated entities. The IRS does require S-Corporation owners that actively participate in the business to pay themselves a "reasonable" salary, on which employment taxes will be paid.

Since it is a pass through entity, any remaining earnings and profits will be picked up as income by the shareholders, taxable on the personal 1040, Schedule E via a Schedule K-1 form. Also passed through are Net Operating Losses, which can be deducted from other income on the personal tax return. If the loss of the S-Corp is greater than the other income of the shareholder, the loss can be carried forward to future tax years on the shareholders personal taxes.

> **Fun fact:** This was how Donald Trump avoided taxes for many years. In the early 1990's, Trump's Casinos had an NOL of $1 billion. The companies were S-Corporations passing through that $1 billion NOL to his personal return which he carried forward for years, canceling out his taxable income.
>
> At the same time, however, the companies filed for bankruptcy protection wiping out the debt. Up until 2002, an S-Corps bankruptcy did not flow to the personal to wipe out the NOL like it does now. This allowed Trump and many others in the 1990's to wipe off debt from the corporate books in a bankruptcy while using the loss personally.

CHAPTER FOUR

CHOOSING THE RIGHT ENTITY

There are many important factors to consider when choosing an entity, including the state, liability protection, tax rates, owners citizenship, property ownership, employees, industry and so many more. In this chapter we will look at examples which address just two of those factors, which are owning property in a business and the business having foreign owners.

Owning property within an entity can mean many things. This can be Real Estate Investors getting a different entity for each property, or it can mean a business with plant and equipment, furniture and fixtures, a fleet of cars or trucks, inventory and so on. Foreign owners can be a foreign investor buying stock in US companies or it can be a foreign person actually opening a business location in the US. Either way, there are laws and policies which need to be addressed.

Foreign Owners - C-Corp

People from all over the world own and invest in US businesses. If a non-resident wants a business in the US what entity is best? Putting their countries tax laws aside, here is the situation as far as US tax laws are concerned.

As previously stated, S-Corps cannot have foreign owners. LLC? but money distributed to a non-US member from an LLC with default tax status, is subject to what's called "Backup Withholding," which can be 24% or more. The member would need to file a US tax return, as a Non-Resident Alien, to claim a refund. This means they would likely need to apply for an ITIN (Individual Tax ID Number), which is not always an easy process.

This leaves a C-Corporation as the natural choice for most foreign business owners and investors. The C-Corp pays its own taxes at the entity level, and the taxation of any dividends paid to foreign owners will be according to their own country's tax laws.

Please Note: There can be some additional filing requirements needed when corporations have foreign shareholders. Form 5472 needs to be filed by a foreign owner of both disregarded entities (SMLLC) and C-Corporations having foreign shareholders with 25% ownership. In addition, foreign entities doing business in the United States are also required to file the form.

The penalties for non-compliance with the Form 5472 filing requirements can be quite steep and strictly enforced. If a Form 5472 filing requirement exists, a $25,000 fine will be imposed for failure to file, filing late, or filling out the form incorrectly.

Rental Real Estate - LLC

The LLC is the preferred entity for landlords for three main reasons: no self-employment tax on rental income, ease of property transfers, and charging order protections.

Rental Income - Income is broken down by type on the business tax forms, such as regular sales, investment, interest, etc. While income from the regular sales of an LLC is taxed on the members personal tax return and subject to self-employment tax, rental income, though still taxed on the members personal return, is generally exempt from self-employment tax.

> **Please Note:** Active participation in short-term rentals, such as cleaning after every renter, washing and changing linens, emptying garbages, etc, can cause the IRS to reclassify rental income as regular business income, subjecting it to self-employment tax.

Property Transfers - Assets held by corporations generally cannot be moved out of the corporation without a taxable event occurring.

The corporation can sell the property or it can distribute the property, but it will be deemed a taxable sale or a taxable distribution. It's much easier to move property in and out of an LLC than a corporation. Title transfers can be used instead of sales or distributions, meaning no income producing taxable event occurred.

Charging Orders - Just having assets in a business does not protect an owner from personal creditors because the ownership of the company is a personal asset. Courts can force shareholders of corporations to transfer their shares to creditors to satisfy a lien or judgment. However, when it comes to an LLC, personal creditors may be limited to charging orders, depending on the state. Only five states extend charging order protections to a single-member LLC; Alaska, Delaware, Nevada, South Dakota and Wyoming.

Charging orders are liens attached to distributions, not ownership. For example, if a shareholder in a corporation gets sued personally and loses, the creditor can acquire the stock shares, becoming a full shareholder with voting rights. However, if a member in an LLC having charging order protection gets sued, the creditor only has a right to collect against distributions made to that member.

> **Please Note:** Caution when opening a SMLLC for property ownership. First, many states will not offer charging order protection to a SMLLC. Second, since it is disregarded as a separate entity for tax purposes, the member will have to list their LLC owned properties on their personal tax return, Form 1040, Schedule E.

CHAPTER FIVE

FORMATION OF ENTITIES

There are multiple steps involved when forming a business entity. Though some details will differ from state to state and from entity to entity there are enough similarities to discuss them here. When it comes to corporations, LLCs and the limited partnerships, formation documents will be filed with the State's Department of State and agreements signed between the owners. When dealing with a sole proprietorship or general partnership there will be a dba filed with the county in which a business is located, business licensing and agreements.

In order to file taxes for a business, the company has to have a TIN, Taxpayer ID Number. In most cases the TIN will be an EIN, Employer ID Number from the IRS. Sole Proprietors with no employees can just use the owners SSN as the TIN.

Records: Forming, Filing, Operating

No State Registration:

General Partnership - Sign a Partnership Agreement between partners, file a *Certificate of Assumed Name* with the county clerk, obtain an EIN from the IRS

Sole Proprietor - File a *Certificate of Assumed Name* with the county clerk, can use own SSN as EIN until there are employees to hire and pay

State Registration:

Limited Partnership - Sign a Partnership Agreement between partners, file a *Certificate of Limited Partnership* with the state, obtain an EIN from the IRS

LLC - File *Articles of Organization* with the state, obtain an EIN from the IRS, sign an Operating Agreement between members.

Corporations - File *Articles of Incorporation* with the state, obtain an EIN from the IRS, adopt Bylaws and sign a Shareholder Agreement.

CHAPTER SIX

TAXATION OF ENTITIES

Each entity type has differences in the way in which they are taxed. Some entities give flexibility allowing owners to choose the way they are taxed while others are strictly defined and rigid. Knowing the differences in the taxation of entities is important when forming your business because choices made at the beginning can be difficult to undo if at all.

This book addresses Federal Income Tax, but there are many taxes that businesses need to file and pay, such as: Franchise, payroll, sales, capital gains, property, excise, highway use, licensing fees, unemployment, workers compensation, and more.

Sole Proprietor (and SMLLC)

Files and pays taxes on the personal tax return of the owner Form 1040, Schedule C and Schedule SE for self-employment taxes.

Partnership (and LLC)

Files a business tax return on Form 1065, computing the profits of the business. The profits are broken down by partner (member) on Schedules K-1, based on their share of the profits of the business. The K-1 is attached onto the personal returns of the partners Forms 1040, Schedule E. Also, Schedule SE for self-employment taxes on the partners share of profits.

S-Corporation

Files business tax return on Form 1120-S. The results are computed per shareholder who receives Schedule K-1. The K-1 attaches to Form 1040, Schedule E. No self-employment taxes. Shareholders actively participating in the business are expected to take a "reasonable salary."

C-Corporation

Files and pays its own tax on Form 1120. If distributing post-tax profits to its shareholders, Forms 1099-DIV are issued and attached to the shareholders personal Form 1040, Schedule B.

Double Taxation - Income taxes are paid by the corporation, and distributions of the post-tax profits are taxed again as income to the shareholder.

IRS Elections

C-Corporations can file an S-Corp election, Form 2553 electing to be taxed as an S-Corporation.

LLC can file an Entity Election on Form 8832 electing to be taxed as a corporation. It has been decided that an LLC electing to be taxed as an S-Corporation, can opt out of filing Form 8832 and instead file Form 2553 directly, rather than having to file both elections.

CHAPTER SEVEN

MULTI-ENTITY FORMATION

Why pick just one? Who wants to settle for Snap, Crackle with out the Pop, or just Crackle and Pop with no Snap? Oftentimes, it would be beneficial to have multiple entities for different functions of business. If done properly, a mix of entities can be used to take advantage of the benefits of each entity type, while minimizing the negatives; once again being able to enjoy the full Snap, Crackle and Pop. An entity to run the business, an entity to own and manage property and assets, an entity to employ employees, and so on.

Different states can be used depending on Nexus, which is a fancy legal word for state residency.

When using multiple business entities, each entity must stand on its own as far as purpose, function, and reasonableness to justify its existence. If the only purpose for an entity is to reduce taxes, the IRS has the ability to disregard the entity or collapse multiple entities into one.

Case-study: Vendor Center

Background

A family called me in to advise them on the tax implications of opening their home goods business. They spoke to their CPA to have him open an LLC as that seems to be the most popular entity these days. The CPA explained an LLC would provide them limited liability and was more simple than a corporation in formation and taxation. A corporation? They had never considered that. In comes me offering this family the full Snap, Crackle and Pop.

Results

Vendor Center seems like a regular store selling home goods and other items. The Sign over the door is Vendor Center, the customer receipts say Vendor Center, even the store charge card says Vendor Center.

While that is all true, Vendor Center Inc does not own anything, not the building, not the products being sold, nor does it employ anyone even though the workers uniforms say Vendor Center. Vendor Center Inc is the operating company, public face and brand, as well as collector of the money.

The Entities

VENDOR CENTER INC Main Company - Corp 1 (C-Corp)

ASSET MANAGER LLC Property Holder- LLC1 (MMLLC)

LABOR FOR RENT LLC Labor Company - LLC2 (SMLLC)

ITS FOR SALE CORP Inventory Company - Corp2 (S-Corp)

FAMILY HOLDINGS FLP Holding Company LP1 (FLP)

Details

Vendor Center pays rent to Asset Manager LLC, which in turn pays the mortgage and property taxes. The weekly paychecks handed out to the workers at Vendor Center are made payable from Labor for Rent LLC, which charges monthly fees to their customer Vendor Center Inc. All of the products being sold at Vendor Center are being sold on consignment, loaned by Its for Sale Corp which purchases and owns all of the products being sold. Its for Sale Corp handles all of the buying, shipping and logistics.

All four companies are owned by the same person, persons or holding company. In this case they are owned by family members through a Family Limited Partnership organized as a holding company.

See Appendix F: Multi-Entity Diagrams for example

PART II

TAX REDUCTION

CHAPTER EIGHT

UNDERSTANDING TAX REDUCTION

"If you don't claim it, you don't get it."
--Mark Everson, Former IRS Commissioner

The government has built into the tax code many ways to reduce your tax burden, and a little planning goes a long way. The government publishes their statutes and laws in the US Code, the tax code being Title 26 of the US Code. They also put out publications broken down by subject matter, some of which are listed on the Works Cited page in the back of the book. The way the government sees it, they have provided the information needed for people to minimize their tax burden, and it's not their fault if people don't read it.

Loopholes or Incentives?

What many refer to as loopholes in the tax law are really better understood as incentives. The United States government uses the tax code for many things other than raising revenue to run the government. The tax code is used to deliver social programs to those in need, such as the Covid stimulus checks, healthcare and more. It's also used to reinforce public policy by incentivizing behavior the government wants to encourage and disincentivizing behavior the government wants to discourage. Examples of incentivizing vs disincentivizing includes: allowing tax breaks for home ownership while offering nothing to renters, and unreimbursed business expenses incurred by a business owner or self-employed contractor are tax deductible, while the unreimbursed expenses of employees are no longer deductible.

> **Important:** Employees should consider whether they are eligible for 1099 contractor status and if it would be advantageous for them to work with their employer to reclassify them as such. Professions requiring traveling to clients, such as traveling nurses, social workers or counselors, will incur expenses related to their vehicles that are no longer deductible as an employee.

Incentives to help others

The following is a personal story I encountered preparing taxes, showing how the IRS encourages behavior that can benefit society as well as result in tax savings. In 2013, I was running the VITA program, an IRS volunteer tax preparation program, for Brooklyn College in Brooklyn, NY, and one experience in particular has always stayed with me. I was preparing a tax return for a professor who is originally from Africa. When we got to the itemizing of deductions, she didn't want to take the deduction for charitable giving. Being as deeply religious as she was, she seemed to think it was sinful to get a financial reward for charity. I explained that the government is incentivizing the giving of charity by allowing the deduction. She wasn't convinced.

Then I said, if she took the deduction it would allow her to give more to charity. The government is subsidizing her donation, so instead of writing a check for $1,000, make it $1,250. She liked the idea and took the deduction. About two weeks later I received an email thanking me, explaining how she thought about what I said, and it inspired her to purchase and donate a water filtration system for her home village in Africa. She would allow the government to help her pay for it.

Income Splitting

Since personal income is taxed at a graduated rate, being able to split off income under another entity is beneficial, as it can allow for a taxpayer to pay taxes at the lower rates of a lower income bracket. It is also possible to take money out of your company in different ways, other than salary, with better tax treatment such as payments made for rent or reimbursement of expenses. Other ways of taking money out of a corporation are the payment of fees as a member of the board of directors, shareholder loans at market interest rates, as well as dividend or non-dividend distributions.

Profit Shifting

When opening business entities, it's often possible to open that entity in a different state than the owner resides. With the correct business entity in the correct state, the business can pay lower state business taxes or even claim residence in a state with no state income or sales tax. Legal residence in a state is determined by different factors and is covered under the legal concept of Nexus. Even when claiming residence in a particular state, you may need to file "non-resident" tax returns in other states in which business was conducted. There are times when being taxed by multiple states can be avoided. Then, there are times you will need to pay the taxes in one state and apply for a credit in another.

Multi-Entity Structuring

As discussed in Part I, it may be beneficial to have multiple entities, as opposed to fitting unrelated businesses or unrelated business activities under one entity. If done properly, a mix of entities can be used to take advantage of the benefits of each entity type, while minimizing any negatives. For example, using a SMLLC or LLC with a married couple as the only members, they can employ their children tax free and charge their main business as a customer. Another LLC can be used to own assets and lease them to your main corporation. The entities all have to be opened and run correctly and have a reason to exist besides tax reduction. If not, the IRS can collapse all the entities into one entity and apply that restructuring retroactively.

Chapter Nine

Tax Avoidance Done Wrong

Offshore Shelters: A Cautionary Tale

The second tax reduction book I ever read was *Offshore Money Havens* by Jerome Schneider in 2001. The book was about forming and owning offshore banks. To minimize Americans using foreign companies to defer their US taxes, rules were created taxing US shareholders on their share of the profits of "controlled" foreign companies, having mostly US owners *(IRC 951)*. However, an exemption was given to foreign banks with US owners *(IRC 954(h))*. In many countries it is surprisingly easy and inexpensive to open a bank, especially compared to the requirements of opening a bank in the US.

After a 30-year career helping his clients avoid taxes, in 2002 Schneider was indicted for conspiracy to defraud the United States, as well as mail and wire fraud. So how did it go so wrong? According to the indictment, Schneider helped his clients hide their ownership of the "banks" they had opened. This seems counterintuitive since the entire purpose of the bank ownership was to have nontaxable income, which is income that can be reported but not taxed. There should have been no reason to hide the ownership.

Reading through the requirements for the tax exemption, the banks needed to be "actively engaged" in banking business. It is not a one and done lifetime exemption but an annual exemption based on the active conduct of business for the year. Even though on paper the foreign companies he helped form were banks, that is all they were, banks on paper. Schneider and his clients merely filled out the forms, but weren't actually engaging in banking activities, such as taking deposits or making loans. To make matters worse, they created legal documents signing over ownership of the banks to a fictitious anonymous foreign investor.

48

When Jerome Schneider was writing books, leading seminars, or giving classes on tax avoidance, he was dealing in the theoretical. In practice, however, the requirements were such, that qualifying every year as an active bank were extremely difficult since there really was no bank. While continuing to preach foreign bank ownership as the ultimate tax avoidance structure, in reality, they were all just evading taxes by hiding their money from the IRS. In fact, reading through the indictment, the case focused on the hiding of the ownership of the foreign banks not whether or not the banks qualified as banks.

Lessons Learned

1. Tax Shelters protect income, not hide income.

2. Report all assets and income that are reportable.

3. Fulfill all the requirements to keep tax preferred assets and income, tax preferred.

Anyone can evade taxes by illegally hiding assets and income, there is nothing special in that. The goal should be avoiding taxes by showing the asset or income that has been legally sheltered.

CHAPTER TEN

BUSINESS RENT EXPENSE

Rent can often be one of the largest expenses a business incurs. It is usually a fixed expense due every month whether or not any business was conducted. Rent can be for a store front, a professional office, a desk inside an office, a chair in a beauty salon, a station at a mechanics garage, and yes, even a Home Office. Rent can also be short term rentals, like Airbnb, for meetings, networking events, team building retreats and company parties.

Rent expense can include short term rentals, like Airbnb, for meeting space, networking events, team building retreats and company parties. Expenses for equipment rentals, storage space, as well as car rentals would also be deducted under rent.

Business Use of Home

When operating a home business as a self-employed sole proprietorship, a portion of personal rent (or mortgage interest, property tax, insurance, depreciation) can be written off for the portion of space used for the business. A sole proprietorship cannot deduct home office rent if the business has a loss.

In order for the home office to qualify for a deduction, there needs to be a particular space in the home used regularly and exclusively for business. This space can be used for doing work, seeing clients, or simply as storage. The deduction would equal the general expenses of the home apportioned for the percentage of space of the home used for the business plus the full expenses particular to the home office itself. *(587, p 3)*

On the Form 1040, Schedule C, the home office deduction would not be taken under office expenses or rent. After all of the income and expenses are entered to get a tentative profit or loss, the home office can be addressed since the deduction cannot be used for a loss. Form 8829, Business Use of your Home is attached to the Schedule C. *(334, p 37)*

Business Pays Owner Rent

When operating a business from your home that is taxed as a corporation, the business would pay the owner rent for the use of the owners residence. The rental expense may be deducted on the business return without regard to profit or loss. The landlord/ business owner must report the rental income on their personal tax return Form 1040, Schedule E, where the rental/ownership expenses would be deducted from the rental income. This should result in a deduction on the business return and a break even on the personal return.

The "Augusta Rule"

If, however, the business is only using the owners home part-time such as for meetings or networking events, if it is less than 15 days of the tax year, the rental income does not need to be reported as income on the personal tax return. The rent expense can still be deducted on the business tax return when done correctly. When using this short-term rental method, rental rates can be in line with the higher rental rates equivalent to Airbnb rates, much higher than normal long-term rentals. This is referred to as the "Augusta Rule," named for the annual golf tournament by that name in Augusta, Georgia.

CHAPTER ELEVEN

SALARY REDUCTION

Employers may provide employees certain benefits to increase the employees compensation without increasing their taxable income. Though not taxable, the employer may still deduct the benefits on the business tax return and the amount is listed on the employees W-2.

Business owners and the self-employed can deduct work related expenses, as long as they are ordinary, necessary, and reasonable. Unfortunately, unreimbursed business expenses are no longer deductible by W-2 employees. However, employers may be able to reimburse their employees for the expenses under an Accountable Plan, which is treated in a similar way as employee benefits.

Fringe Benefits

Benefit plans are a good way for employers to provide non-taxable compensation to their employees. Some examples of non taxable compensation are employer paid health insurance, retirement plans, medical expenses, child care expenses, education, parking, etc. Benefits create regular deductible expenses for the business while offering tax-free payments to the employee. Be careful, there are stipulations specific to the benefit type.

<u>Stipulations</u>:

Official Policy - The plan details must be in writing in the company's policy as well as written in the employment agreements.

Payment Method - Payment from the company can be made beforehand as a per diem or even a direct prepayment, done through an expense account used by the employee, or reimbursed after the fact upon employee request with receipts.

Non-Discrimination - Some benefits must be offered to all employees. Without this rule companies would give special plans to executives. Companies could lose the tax benefits if they discriminate against a class of worker.

Worker Status - Partners and 1099 independent contractors generally do not qualify for fringe benefits. Employee benefits are just for employees. This means that members in an LLC and partners in a partnership may not be able to take advantage of these benefits.

Entity Type - Different entity types qualify for different benefits and have different requirements. C-Corporations are allowed the most tax free and tax preferred benefits as a way to ease the double taxation unique to C-Corps.

Retirement Plans

There are tax benefits to the employee and employer for retirement accounts. Generally speaking, employees can invest with pre-tax money and the employer can deduct amounts from their taxable income.

There are many choices of retirement plans, all with different limits and requirements, some done by the employer and some done by oneself. There are special retirement accounts for the self-employed taxpayer that offer tremendous benefits to a population that usually goes underrepresented when it comes to retirement planning. Here are two plans often used by the self-employed, the Solo 401(k) and the SEP IRA.

Solo 401(k) - A retirement account for the self-employed person with no employees, or minimal part-time employees. A self-directed solo 401(k) gives the person complete control over the investments, and may allow for alternative investments not available to other retirement plans. The plan can engage in private lending, own real estate, precious metals, tax liens, crypto and more.

The contribution limits are higher than other retirement options as the plan allows the self-employed person to contribute to the plan as an employee and as an employer. There is also the ability to borrow against the plan, instead of making taxable withdrawls.

SEP IRA - Self-employed people can open a SEP whether or not they have employees. If the business does have employees, they must be covered under the plan as well. SEP IRAs have lower startup costs and higher contribution limits than other plans.

Accountable Plans

Sometimes known as a reimbursement plan or an expense account, it is a good way to deal with the loss of the unreimbursed employee expense deduction. Qualifying expenses can be office supplies, transportation, uniforms, tools, etc.

Similar to benefit plans in the way they are taxed, accountable plans have different requirements. The three stipulations that need to be met inorder to maintain the tax benefits are:

- Expense has a business purposes, by an employee, while working,
- evidence is given to the employer,
- the employee cannot keep the change.

CHAPTER TWELVE

TRAVEL: BUSINESS OR PERSONAL

An often asked question, "Can I write off a personal vacation as a business expense?" Most tax experts say "No! Of course not," but in reality, it depends. If you understand the business travel tax rules you can adjust your real-world situation to fit inside the rules. Tax planning is used to set things up in advance to get a tax deduction while staying in compliance with the tax laws.

When traveling for business, only "business days" are deductible, meaning days spent conducting business. "Tax experts" say you cannot deduct personal days and they would need to be apportioned with business days for the deduction. With tax law, however, things are often different from how they appear and written to purposely confuse.

What Qualifies as a Business Day?

Business days are days in which business is conducted, planned, discussed or learned about. Travel days and weekends can also be business days when necessary for business purposes. In further detail, business days are:

Business days - Days in which business is conducted for at least four hours qualify,

Travel days - As long as the destination is for business, the days spent traveling to and from qualify,

Weekends when necessary - As long as you conduct business on Friday and will be conducted on that following Monday, staying over Saturday and Sunday qualify. The destination has to be far enough away from your work home that it makes back and forth travel unreasonable. *(463, p 8)*

Domestic vs International

There are differences in the law depending on whether the business travel is domestic or international. For all business travel you need to apportion expenses between business days and personal days. However, there is an exception to the apportionment rules when traveling outside the US for business. If the entire trip, beginning the day after departing the US and ending when landing back in the US, is one week or less it is assumed that every day is a business day and is therefore exempt from the apportionment requirements. *(463, p 7)*

Tax Optimized Travel Itinerary

Thursday - Travel to destination

Friday - Four hours of business

Weekend - Whatever you want

Monday- Four hours of business

Tuesday - Travel back home

As long as proper records are kept, a minimum of eight hours of work can net a maximum of six days of business travel deductions. Now, answer the question, can a vacation be tax deductible?

Life Hack: Annual Meeting TBD

A great feature, unique to a Corporation is that it is legally required to have at least one meeting per year. One can choose to set up that meeting to coincide with a vacation, thereby giving the travel a business purpose.

In the bylaws of the corporation, there are sections for different types of meetings. Regular board meetings, annual board meetings as well as annual shareholders meetings. Language should be inserted for the time and place to be determined at a later time upon notice. This means the meetings can be held whenever and wherever desired.

A notice, agenda and minutes of the meeting are all required. The minutes are records of business matters discussed or considered, with date, time, and those attended. The meeting, as well as required documentation, are still required, even if the entire company is made up of one person.

CHAPTER THIRTEEN

HIRING FAMILY MEMBERS

There are actually tax breaks offered for hiring immediate family members. The tendency for the tax code to encourage family businesses may be the remanence of a simpler time when family businesses were a bedrock of American society. Families were able to bridge multiple generations passing the businesses down, allowing families to build wealth and status over time. *(15, p 13)*

Employing Spouse

Benefits as payment- There is limited direct tax savings from issuing a spouse a paycheck. The tax breaks come from replacing regular wages with tax free and tax preferred employee benefit plans. In an audit the IRS could ask for proof of actual work having been done by the spouse. The monetary value of the benefit plan cannot be too unreasonable considering the amount of work performed. Be careful, this strategy is highly dependent on the entity type as well as coverage for other employees.

Qualifies for Child Care <u>Credit</u> - When parents send their children to daycare, day camp or hire babysitters, they may be able to qualify for a tax credit. In order for a married couple filing taxes jointly to claim the Child and Dependent Care Credit both spouses need to be working. Employing an unemployed spouse makes the couple eligible to claim the credit as long as the other requirements are met.

Qualifies for Child Care <u>Benefit</u> - The business can pay for the childcare from the business account, gaining a deductible expense for the business and giving tax free money to your spouse or employee. This eliminates the need and ability to claim the dependent care credit on the personal return. *(15-B, p 9)*

Employing Owners Children

The standard deduction for 2022 per individual taxpayer is $12,950. This makes it possible to pay your child up to that amount per year providing tax free income to your children while giving your business that extra tax deduction. In addition, the owners children under age 18 are also exempt from employment taxes. Thresholds for minimum age and work aren't strictly defined, but the child needs to engage in "meaningful tasks." Photocopying, stuffing envelopes and emptying trash are all meaningful tasks a 4-year-old can probably do. *(15, p 13)*

Some business owner-parents use employing their children as a way to give an allowance while

67

instilling work ethic and financial literacy. Others use it as a way to generate tax free money to invest in tax preferred education funds for the child.

Entities to Employ Children

The entity type from which children are paid is important. Children do not receive the payroll tax exemption when paid from a corporation. The only entities that qualify are:

Sole proprietor owned by either parent,

Partnership where the parents are the only partners,

SMLLC in which either parent is the member, and

LLC in which the parents are the only members.

Kiddie Tax and Filing Requirement

Be careful not to trigger the "Kiddie Tax" or a general filing requirement for the child. The parents need to anticipate and account for any other income the child will have for the year.

General Filing Requirement - The child can earn regular wages up to the standard deduction, $12,950 for 2022 without having to file. If other income is reported, from a part time job, interest, etc bringing the child's AGI above that, or has $400 in net self-employment income, the child will have to file a return.

Kiddie Tax - When a child's unearned income, like interest, dividends and capital gains, is over $1,150, a filing requirement gets triggered, though the parents can choose to file it on their return using Form 8615, Tax for Certain Children Who Have Unearned Income.

Combining Strategies: Employing Family and Business Travel

Employing family members can mean more flexibility as far as deducting meals, vacations, phones and company vehicles, since they aren't just family anymore; they are employees. Remember that expenses need to be ordinary, necessary, and reasonable.

Instead of having family members as employees, you can have them as shareholders, or even have the family as the Board of Directors. Travel, dinners, parties, etc can be classified as meetings. Notice, agenda and minutes of the meeting are required.

Family Wealth Preservation

Family business structures such as the Family LLC, Family LP and Family Trust are used in estate planning and wealth preservation strategies. Only relatives related by blood, marriage or adoption can be members or partners in these family business entities. The operating agreement, partnership agreement, or trust document will detail the qualifications, requirements and ownership percentages. Sucession plans will also be laid out as well as many other important details.

CHAPTER FOURTEEN

VEHICLE EXPENSE DEDUCTION

Business owners, landlords and the self-employed that use vehicles for business purposes, may deduct the business expenses; employees can no longer do so.*

Like other business related assets, owned vehicles need to be depreciated. However, there are rules specifically written for vehicles.

There are two general methods to figure out deductible vehicle expenses, the standard mileage rate or the actual expense method.

*In order for employees to get relief for expenses they incurred on behalf of the business, a written Reimbursement Plan is needed. The business reimburses the employee and takes the deduction on the business tax return. *See Chapter 10: Salary Reduction*

Standard Mileage Rate

The standard mileage rate is supposed to represent the general costs of owning and operating a vehicle broken down on a per mile basis. The rate fluctuates from year to year with 65.5 Cents per business mile as the 2023 rate. About 25 out of the 65 cents represents depreciation. *(463, p 14)*

> **Please Note:** Business miles do not include commuting miles, which are defined as home to work and work to home.

To use the standard mileage rate, you must do so from the first year the vehicle is available for use in your business. If leased, using the standard rate for the first year means using it for the entire lease; if the vehicle is owned, actual expenses can be chosen in a later year.

Parking fees and tolls - In addition to using the standard mileage rate, business-related parking and tolls can be deducted as well.

> **Please Note:** Parking fees you pay to park your car at your main place of work are non-deductible commuting expenses.

Actual Vehicle Expenses

Ownership expenses such as Depreciation, Interest, Lease payments, Insurance.

Operating expenses such as Gas, Oil, Repairs, Garage, as well as Parking and tolls. *(463, p 15)*

Deduction vs Depreciation

Expenses are deducted the year they are incurred. Expenses for vehicles are gasoline, insurance, repairs, et al. Lease payments are deducted but finance payments are not, since a purchased vehicle is an asset, not an expense.

Assets are depreciated over multiple years. In other words, assets are partially deducted each year until the full value has been written off. There are different methods of depreciation, which are beyond the scope of this book.

Useful Life - The number of years an asset is expected to be economically viable before it needs replacing. For example, office furniture has a useful life of seven years, equipment and computers are five years, as are vehicles. The depreciation recovery period is set to the useful life of the asset.

In general, the tax deductible amount of depreciation on a vehicle is based on the purchase price broken down over five years, starting from the time the car is available for use in your business. The actual process for computing depreciation is of course more complicated, but again, beyond the scope of this book.

First Year Depreciation

There are tax incentives allowing businesses to take more depreciation in the year assets are purchased.

Expensing - Section 179 of the tax code allows for Accelerated Depreciation which allows for taking a higher depreciation deduction in the first year, depending on the vehicle class.

Bonus Depreciation - Section 168(k) of the tax code allows for a special depreciation election on top of the 179 deduction. This had the potential of allowing a deduction up to the full price for both new and used vehicles. Unfortunately, the election is being slowly phased out over the next three years, starting with 2023 at 80%. *(946, p 18)*

Vehicle Class

GVWR - Every vehicle has a set Gross Vehicle Weight Rating. This weight is equal to the actual weight plus the safe capacity weight of fuel, passengers and cargo. Vehicle class is mainly based on the GVWR.

Car - any four-wheeled vehicle (car, SUV, van, truck) made primarily for use on public streets with a gross vehicle weight of 6000 lbs or less.

Heavy SUV - A four-wheeled vehicle between 6001 and 14,000 lbs GVWR.

Heavy Truck - A vehicle over 14,000 lbs GVWR.

Special Use Vehicles - Referred to in the tax code as Qualified Nonpersonal Use Vehicles and are less likely to be used for personal purposes. This includes taxis, hearses, ambulances, limited seating delivery trucks and more. Also included are specially modified vehicles, such as vans, with installed permanent shelves and the company name painted on the vehicle. *(946, p 18)*

Rules for First Year Depreciation

More than 50% business use - You must use the vehicle more than 50% for business to claim any section 179 deduction. Multiply the cost of the property by the percentage of business use. The result is the cost that can qualify for the Section 179 deduction.

Order of operations - Determine vehicle class, figure business use, Section 179 deduction, then special 168k, and anything left over could qualify for regular depreciation over 5 years.

Basis for depreciation - Subtract the amount of the 179 and special depreciation to figure the amount you can claim in regular depreciation.

Timing - Both the section 179 deduction and special bonus depreciation must be elected on the tax return, in the tax year the vehicle was placed in service for business.

Form to use - Form 4562, Depreciation and Amortization, to make the election.

Documentation - A mileage log must be maintained and provided to the IRS if requested.

Depreciation Limitations

Conversion - Vehicles used for personal purposes do not qualify for the extra depreciation in a later year when its use changes to business.

Vehicle bought and sold in same year - You can not claim any depreciation deduction for a vehicle placed in service and disposed of in the same tax year.

Recapture of Section 179 deduction - If the business use of a vehicle falls below 50% for a tax year within the "recovery period" in this case, four years of claiming the 179 deduction, the "extra depreciation" will be recaptured and picked up as income. Selling the vehicle can also lead to picking up more income as the extra depreciation can lead to a larger than normal gain on the sale. *(946, p 22)*

Business and personal use - When using a vehicle for both business and personal purposes, expenses must be allocated between business and personal use based on the miles driven for each purpose. Ideally, your mileage log should only have business miles listed.

Profit Limitation on Section 179

The total amount you can deduct under Section 179 each year "...is limited to the taxable income from the active conduct of any trade or business during the year."

This is a very misunderstood provision because many falsely believe you need to earn a profit in the business in which you use the vehicle, but when you understand the wording "...conduct of ANY trade or business...," it means something very different. Losing money in a business does not stop you from claiming the 179 deduction, as long as you are making enough money in other businesses or even as a W-2 employee to cover the business loss plus the deduction. Any deduction not taken due to this limitation, may be carried forward to future years. *(946, p 19)*

Limits and Exemptions by Class

The 2023 tax year dollar limit on a Section 179 deduction for a car is $12,200 and $28,900 for a heavy SUV.

Exemptions to the dollar limitation for any vehicle that has:

- A seating capacity of more than nine persons behind the driver's seat;

- An outside cargo area of at least 6 feet in length and isn't readily accessible directly from the passenger compartment; or

- A fully enclosed driver compartment, doesn't have seats behind the driver, and has a short front body.

More Deductions and Limitations

Interest Deduction - Financing a business vehicle using the proceeds from a home equity loan, may allow for a deduction on interest paid.

State Personal Property Tax - Allocate the deduction for the tax expense between business and personal if itemizing on Form 1040, Schedule A.

Tickets - Fines paid for parking or moving violations can not be deducted.

PART III

APPENDICES

Appendix A

Six Starter Businesses

Here are six business ideas with low startup costs, no licensing or certification needed, and only requiring minimal time and effort. These businesses practically run themselves while generating profits for you.

Affiliate Marketing

A kind of referral service for other companies' products or services. Your business is to earn commission by connecting the product or service provider with customers. Whether that means actively selling, a click-through banner on a website or a post on social media, you are making money by helping other companies make money.

Drop Shipping

This is selling products on the internet without having to stock inventory or ship orders. You would register with a manufacturer or distributor as a dealer and sell products online or on the phone. You collect the payment and information, then send the customer information to the distributor that fulfills the order. You remit payment to the distributor at the dealer price, keeping the difference.

Outsourcing

This is similar to drop shipping, but with services as opposed to products. You would charge for services and then hire out a service provider at a lower rate. For instance, being that the national minimum wage is under $8 but $15 in New York, one can outsource work to a different state at a lower rate. There are even websites with service providers from all over the world.

Digital Marketing

This is posting content on social media for customers, SEO and web ads. If you are someone that enjoys being on social media posting content and interacting with followers, digital marketing may be a great fit for you.

Marketplace Seller

This is drop shipping 2.0, where the marketplace is handling additional processes normally taken care of by the distributors. The benefit over traditional drop shipping is the sales platform comes with. If you choose to have the marketplace store and fulfill the sales like drop shipping, it can be a very hands off process. For those that want to keep more on each sale, taking on the storage and shipping is the way to go, though can be labor intensive depending on the products. Most of the marketplaces will also handle the withholding, remitting, and filing of sales taxes for you.

Insourcing

Being a service provider or freelancer on websites like Fiverr and Upwork. Instead of hiring out workers to do tasks for you, be the worker getting hired to do the tasks. If you have a knack for something, why not rent out your services and get paid for your abilities. Some people even offer out their services doing what they do all day at work. If that is something you can do, that will be the greatest way of starting your first side business. Some worry about taking the leap into freelancing or business ownership and here is a perfect way to transition. Though some use the websites to hirer foreigners for less money, many don't feel comfortable with that and prefer someone closer to home and are willing to pay more.

Appendix B
Sample Certificate of Incorporation

When forming a corporation with the state, the filer would list the name, county, address and stock shares authorized. The state will then issue a Certificate of Incorporation based on that information.

Here is a sample for YOUR BUSINESS INC:

CERTIFICATE OF INCORPORATION
OF
YOUR BUSINESS INC
Under Section 402 of the Business Corporation Law

1. The name of the corporation is:

YOUR BUSINESS INC

2. This corporation is formed to engage in any lawful activity for which a corporation may be organized under the Business Corporation Law...

3. The county in which the corporate office is to be located is Your County.

4. The corporation shall have authority to issue:
200 SHARES WITH NO PAR VALUE.

5. The Secretary of State is designated as agent of process. The address to which the Secretary shall mail a copy of any process against the corporation:

STREET ADDRESS

I certify that I have read the above statements, I am authorized to sign this Certificate of Incorporation, that the above statements are correct and that my signature typed below constitutes my signature.

Signed by Incorporator

Appendix C

Sample Bylaws of the Corporation

After the state approves the Articles of Incorporation or issues a Certificate of Incorporation, the Incorporator calls a Shareholders meeting with potential Directors. At the meeting, they will nominate and vote for a Board of Directors, adopt the corporate bylaws, appoint officers, pass resolutions, and other duties necessary and proper in the legal formation of a corporation.

For tax reduction purposes, the important clauses are the required meetings, compensation for directors including traveling expenses to the meetings, existence of other offices besides the main office. It's also important to state that one person can hold all positions.

Here are sample bylaws for our company,
YOUR BUSINESS INC

CORPORATE BYLAWS OF
YOUR BUSINESS INC

ARTICLE 1. CORPORATION

1.1 <u>Incorporation</u>. YOUR BUSINESS INC (the "Corporation") is a duly authorized corporation...

ARTICLE 2. OFFICES

2.1 <u>Registered Office</u>. Main location at which business is conducted.

2.2 <u>Other Offices</u>. May also have offices at such other places, both within and out of the State

ARTICLE 3. STOCKHOLDERS' MEETINGS

3.1 <u>Place of Meetings</u>. Meetings of the stockholders may be held, at such place, in or out of State as may be determined by the Board.

3.2 <u>Annual Meeting</u>. Annual meeting of the stockholders shall be held on a date and time as may be designated by the Board.

3.3 <u>Special Meetings</u>. (a) Special meetings of the stockholders of the Corporation may be called, for any purpose.

3.4 <u>Notice of Meetings</u>. When shareholders can vote at a meeting, a written notice will be sent to shareholders entitled to vote.

ARTICLE 4. DIRECTORS

4.6 <u>Meetings</u>. Meetings of the Board may be called by any director or the President upon notice specifying the purpose of meeting.

4.9 <u>Compensation</u>. Directors are entitled to compensation as approved by the Board, including expenses of attendance.

ARTICLE 5. OFFICERS

5.1 <u>Officers</u>. The Officers include: (a) the President; (b) the Secretary and (c) the Treasurer. One person may hold multiple offices.

Appendix D
Business Mileage Log

Whether choosing the Standard Mileage Rate or the Actual Expense method, the business mileage needs to be tracked. If the IRS questions the business mileage claimed on a tax return, a mileage log is what they want to see. The log should have dates, miles, business purpose and even odometer readings.

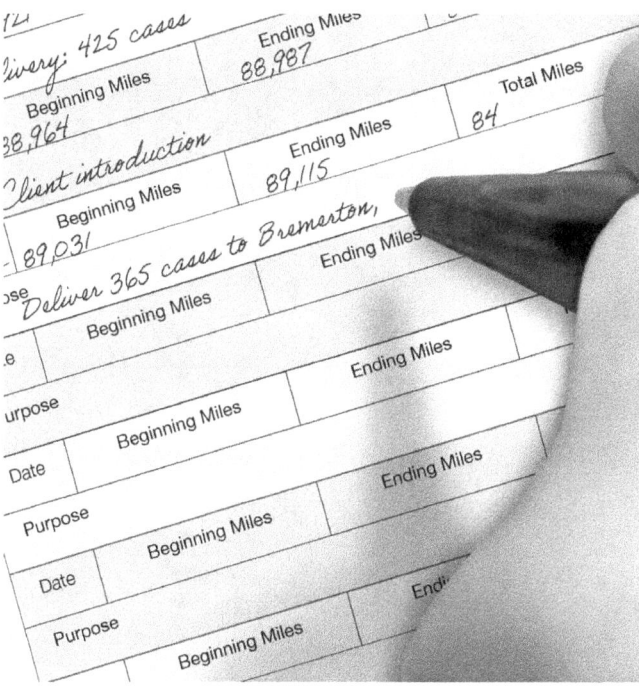

Appendix E

Entity Comparison Chart

Entity type is among the first business decisions a small business owner has to make. Often this step is not given the attention it deserves. Once the entity is formed it can be difficult to change. It is important to understand the different entity types and what conditions are right for each.

	Sole Prop	Partnership
State Registration	No	No
Transferability	No	Yes
Personal Liability	Yes	Yes
Double Tax	No	No
Pass Through	Yes	Yes
Self-Employment Tax	Yes	Yes
Tax Forms	1040, Sch C	1065

LLC	S-Corp	C-Corp
Yes	Yes	Yes
Yes	Yes	Yes
No	No	No
No	No	Yes
Yes	Yes	No
Yes	No	No
Depends	1120S	1120

1. Partnership is based on a General Partnership
2. By default, SMLLC files on Sch C and MMLLC on 1065
3. LLC's may also choose to file on 1120 and 1120S

APPENDIX F
MULTI-ENTITY DIAGRAMS

The main two reasons for forming multiple entities are asset protection and tax reduction. The following diagrams are based on a person owning a business as well as the building in which it is located. The client had asked me if they should have the office building in their name or the business name. I gave them a third and fourth option.

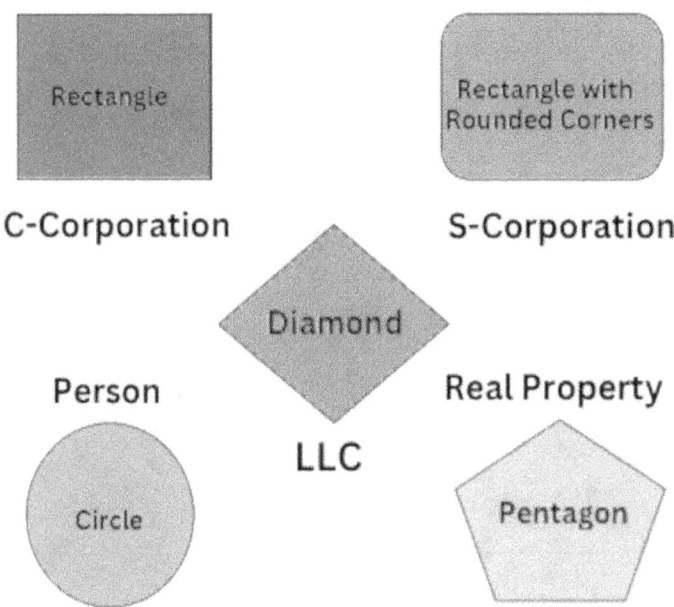

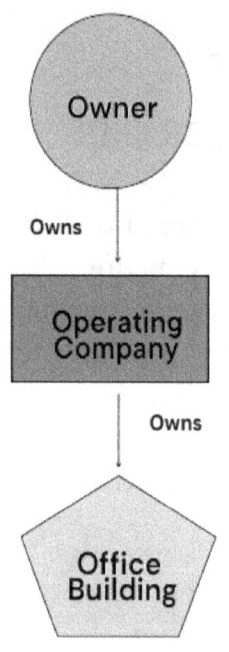

Figure F2 - (Left) Owner has personal asset protection against the building but does not have business asset protection. Creditors of the business can still come after the property.

No tax benefit.

Figure F3 - (Below) Owner has business asset protection against the building but not personal asset protection.

Tax benefit from lease arrangement and income splitting.

Fig F3

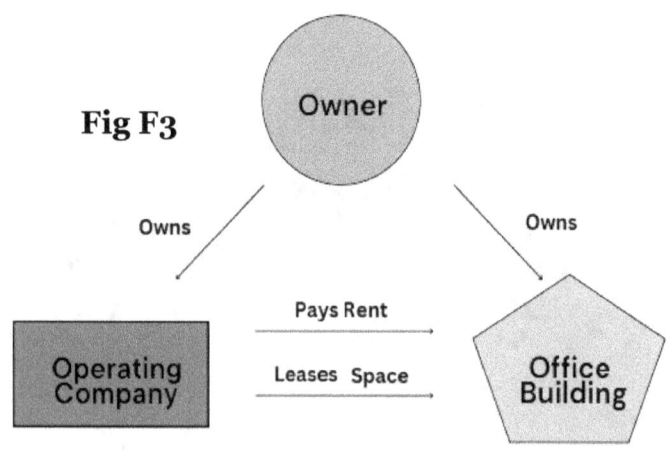

Figure F4 - Owner has business and personal asset protection against the building.

Tax benefit from lease arrangement and income splitting.

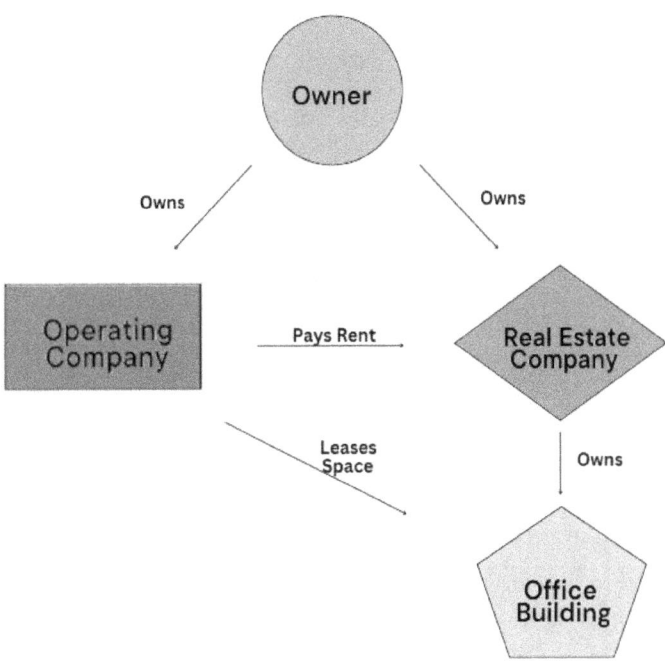

Figure F5 - Owner completely seperate from the businesses and property using a Holding Company, set up as an S-Corporation. A Trust can also be used, though please seek competent legal advice from an experienced attorney who specializes in asset protection trusts.

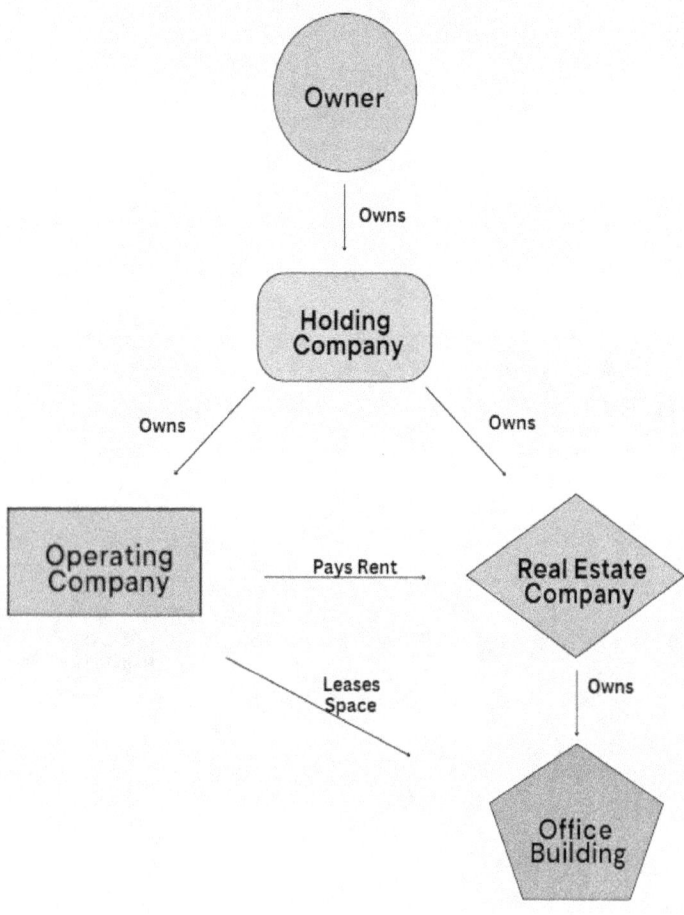

Appendix G
IRS Tax Forms

The most important IRS tax forms for tax paying, business owning, gig working, side-hustlers like you.

Main Forms

1040 - U.S. Individual Income Tax Return

1065 - U.S. Return of Partnership Income

1120 - U.S. Corporation Income Tax Return

1120-S - U.S. Income Tax Return for an S Corporation

990 - Return of Organization Exempt From Income Tax

1041 - U.S. Income Tax Return for Estates and Trusts

Schedules

C - Profit or Loss from Business (Sole Proprietorship)

D - Capital Gains and Losses

E - Supplemental Income and Loss

SE - Self-Employment Tax

Attachment Forms

4562 - Depreciation and Amortization

4797 - Sales of Business Property

8824 - Like-Kind Exchanges

8829 - Expenses for Business Use of Your Home

8582 - Passive Activity Loss Limitations

8949 - Sales and other Dispositions of Capital Assets

5472 - Information Return of a 25% Foreign-Owned...

Election Forms

2553 - Election by a Small Business Corporation

3115 - Application for Change in Accounting Method

1128 - Application to Adopt, Change ... a Tax Year

8832 - Entity Classification Election

Information Returns

1098 - Mortgage Interest Statement

1099-B - Proceeds from Broker ... Transactions

1099-K - Payment Card and Third Party Network...

1099-R - Distributions From Pensions ... Retirement...

K-1 - Share of Income, Deductions, Credits, etc

W-4 - Employee's Withholding Certificate

W-9 - Request for Taxpayer Identification Number...

1099-DIV - Dividends and Distributions

1099-Misc - Miscellaneous Income

1099-NEC - Nonemployee Compensation

GLOSSARY

Accrual Basis Taxpayer - Accounting recognizing income when it is earned regardless of when it is paid; recognizes expenses when they are incurred regardless of when they are paid.

Actual Expense Method - Deducting vehicle expenses based on the actual expenses of owning and operating the vehicle, apportioned accordingly.

Adjusted Basis - The amount to be recovered through depreciation by taking the cost of an asset, adjusted up or down depending on the facts involved in the specific asset.

Adjusted Gross Income - The income left over after subtracting certain allowed adjustments from the Gross Income.

AGI - See Adjusted Gross Income

Asset - Something of value that is owned by a business or individual to store value or produce income.

Asset Protection - Structuring businesses and entities in a way that makes it more difficult for an owner to lose an asset in a lawsuit or other such thing.

Asset Protection Trust - A legal structure between an owner of an asset and the asset itself.

Augusta Rule - A rule named for the annual golf tournament in Augusta, Georgia, allowing people to rent out space in their home for two weeks without having to report the income as taxable.

Balance Sheet - A financial statement listing the assets, liabilities and equity of a business at a specific point in time.

Basis - See Adjusted Basis; Cost Basis

Benefits - See Employee Benefits

Bonus Depreciation - See Special Depreciation.

Book vs Tax - Two methods of accounting that treat certain transactions differently.

Books - An accounting of income, expenses, profit or loss, and assets, liabilities, and equity.

Business - Activity engaged in to earn a Profit.

Business Day - In this context, a day in which traveling costs are deductible as business expenses. Days that business is conducted, travel days, and certain weekends when necessary. See Chapter 11 - Travel; Business or Personal.

Business Entity - See Legal Entity

Calendar Year - A 12-month period from Jan 1 to Dec 31.

Capital Asset - Assets that generally cannot be fully deducted in the year purchased....

Capital Gain or Loss - The increase or decrease of value when an investment is sold vs when it was bought.

Capital Gains Tax - Tax on the increased value of an investment when sold. Investments held for over one year are usually taxed at a lower rate.

Capitalization - See Depreciation

Car - 4 wheeled vehicle with a GVWR of 6,000 lbs or less.

Cash Basis Taxpayer - Accounting that recognizes income when money is received and recognizes expenses when money is spent.

Certified Public Accountant - An accountant licensed by one of the 50 states in all areas of accounting, who has unlimited practice rights to represent clients before the IRS.

Charging Order - Lien on the distributions of an LLC or limited partnership (LP) for debts of a member or partner.

Charging Order Protection - Limits liability of LLCs, LPs, and their members or partners from the debts of its members or partners. Only 5 states offer these protections to Single Member LLCs.

COGS - See Cost Of Goods Sold.

Commuting - travelling between home and work that are not deductible as travelling expenses.

Contractor - See Subcontractor.

Conversion - An Asset changing from personal to business or business to personal.

Corporation - A legally created organization with all the legal rights of a person, made up of one or more people or entities that own shares.

Cost Basis - Asset cost to be recovered through depreciation.

Cost Of Goods Sold - Generally, the full cost of inventory cannot be deducted, only the cost of the inventory that was actually sold. The formula is begining inventory, plus inventory purchased during the year, minus the ending inventory.

CPA - See Certified Public Accountant.

DBA - See Doing Business As.

Deduction - A reduction in taxable income, which will then reduce the taxes owed.

Depreciation - The costs of assets have to be recovered over multiple years instead of deducted in one year like expenses.

Depreciation Recapture - Paying back the depreciation taken, when disposing of, or converting the asset.

Distributions - Payments made from a business to it's owners that generally affects the Inside Basis of the owner but does not result in taxable Income.

Documentation - proof and evidence to support trans-actions claimed on a tax return.

Doing Business As - Registering to use a different name to conduct business; Trade name.

EA - See Enrolled Agent.

EAMike - Michael J. Hovell, EA

Employee - A regular worker upon who the employer has oversight, control as well as withholds and remits taxes.

Employee Benefits - Amounts provided by an employer in addition to the salary and wages of employees. Benefits generally take the form of health, retirement, or fringe.

Enrolled Agent - A tax accountant enrolled through the IRS who has unlimited practice rights when representing taxpayers before the IRS.

Entity - See Legal Entity.

Equity - The difference between Assets and Liabilities of a company. If a company wanted to sell everything it owns, and pay off everything it owes, how much it has left.

Expense - Money spent in order to keep a business running and producing income.

Expensing - Taking depreciation as a deduction in the first year of owning an asset, under Section 179 of the tax code.

FICA - Federal Insurance Contributions Act. See Payroll Tax.

Fiscal Year - A 12-month period not ending on Dec 31. A business can declare or elect to have their tax liability calculated on a non-calendar year. Ex. July 1 to June 30.

Fringe Benefits - Employers may provide additional tax preferred compensation on top of, and/or instead of wages.

Franchise Tax - State taxes on Business Entities. Can take the form of annual fees and/or taxes on revenue, income, assets, capital, et al.

Gross Income - All of an individual's income, deemed taxable, reported on the personal tax return.

Gross Profit - The amount left over when subtracting the Cost Of Goods Sold from the Gross Receipts.

Gross Receipts - The total Revenue collected by a business before deducting expenses.

Gross Vehicle Weight Rating - This rating, fixed at the vehicle manufacturer, determines the Vehicle Class for tax purposes. The rating consists of the actual curb weight of the vehicle plus the safe capacity of passengers, cargo and fuel.

GVWR - See Gross Vehicle Weight Rating.

Heavy SUV - An SUV with a GVWR between 6,001 lbs and 14,000

Heavy Truck - A truck with a GVWR over 14,000 lbs

Home Office - Conducting business inside the home, may provide tax benefits if set up correctly, by reclassifying personal expenses into business expenses.

Income Shifting - See Profit Shifting.

Income Splitting - Tax Reduction Strategy that splits income among persons and/or entities in order to report lower incomes in a graduated tax system resulting in lower tax rates.

Income Statement - A financial statement listing the revenue and expenses of a business over a specific period of time.

Information Returns - Tax returns filed with IRS and states, and sent to taxpayers providing information on income or expenses.

Inside Basis - The value of the economic investment a Partnership, LLC or Corporation has in the Assets it holds.

Kiddie Tax - When children have unearned income above a set amount, $1,250, the parents can elect to file that on their own return instead of filing a separate return for the child. Unearned income between $1,251 and $2,500 is taxed at the child's rate, and anything above $2,500 is taxed at the parents regular rates.

Legal Entity - Corporations, LLCs and Partnerships are legal creations that are distinct from their owners, can contract in their own name, sue and be sued, and have many of the same rights and privileges as natural people.

Limited Liability - Generally speaking, owners/shareholders of corporations and members of LLCs, are not personally at risk for debts of the business.

Limited Liability Company - A legal creation formed by one or more members which offers a hybrid of Partnerships and Corporations. LLCs are taxed as a Sole-Proprietorship if a Single Member or Partnership if a Multi-Member, but can choose to be taxed as a Corporation.

LLC - See Limited Liability Company.

Loophole - See Tax Incentive.

Loss - See Net Operating Loss.

Meetings - Shareholder, member, board, executive, and other types of meetings may produce tax deductible expenses. Corporations are required to have at least one meeting per year, anywhere they'd like.

Member - An Owner of an LLC.

Members' Basis - See Outside Basis.

Net Operating Loss - A negative profit resulting from having more expenses than income. This negative income can be carried over to another year or passed through to the personal returns of the owners depending on the entity type.

Nexus - Determines what states can and cannot tax a business.

NOL - See Net Operating Loss.

Outside Basis - The value of the economic investment a partner, member or shareholder has in the partnership, LLC or Corporation, which fluctuates over time due to a number of factors and needs to be tracked.

P & L - Profit Loss Statement. See Income Statement.

Partner - A co-owner of a Partnership.

Partners' Basis - See Outside Basis.

Partnership - Unincorporated Pass-Through business owned by more than one person or entity. Partnerships can be General, Limited, Limited Liability, Limited Limited Liability.

Partnership Basis - AKA Inside Basis; The value of the economic investment the Partnership has in the Assets it holds.

Pass-Through Entity - Partnerships, S-corporations and some LLCs that figure their Taxable Income on a business return, which then passes that income through to the owners personal tax returns, either increasing or decreasing their personal taxable income.

Payroll Taxes - A portion of salary that goes into paying Social Security and Medicare taxes, which is paid by both the employee and employer.

Personal Property - Property and assets that are not attached to the land and are mobile.

Profit - The amount of money remaining after subtracting expenses from Revenue.

Profit Loss Statement - See Income Statement.

Profit Shifting - AKA income shifting, moves income or profits to jurisdictions with lower tax rates.

QJV - See Qualified Joint Venture.

QRP - See Qualified Retirement Account.

Qualified Joint Venture - Two spouses owning and/or working as partners in a business that has no Legal Entity can choose to treat the business as two separate Sole Proprietorships, rather than a partnership.

Qualified Nonpersonal Use Vehicle - A vehicle that is not designed for personal use, such as a hearse, ambulance, certain vans and pickup trucks meeting the regulations described in the tax code. They are exempt from the depreciation limits on vehicles.

Qualified Retirement Account - A retirement plan like a 401(k) allowing a tax deduction to the employer while deferring taxes for the employee. Self-employed can qualify as well.

Real Estate - See Real Property.

Real Property - AKA Real Estate. Property and assets that are attached to the land and not movable.

Records - The legal documents of a business, meeting minutes, as well as documentation to prove the accuracy of the books.

Recovery Period - The number of years it take to recover the cost of an asset and generally equals the useful life.

Reimbursement - If set up correctly, employers can reimburse employees for expenses they incurred on behalf of the business. Workers can no longer deduct work expenses directly but can be reimbursed by the business, who will take the deduction on the business return.

S-Corporation - A Corporation which made an election with the IRS under Subchapter S of the tax code to be treated as a Pass-Through Entity.

Salary Reduction - Using Fringe Benefits to provide tax preferred compensation instead of fully taxable salary.

Self-Employed - AKA Sole Proprietor; Working for oneself as both the employer and employee. See Subcontractor;

Self-Employment Taxes - Payroll taxes paid for both the employee and employer portions, which comes out to a little over 15%, on top of income taxes.

Separately Stated Items - In Pass Through Entities, some items of income, expenses, gains and losses may affect the taxable income of individual members, partners or shareholders differently and are therefore stated separately then others.

Shareholder - An owner of a Corporation.

Shareholder Basis - See Outside Basis.

Sole Proprietor - AKA Self-Employed. Unincorporated business, owned by one person that is not separate from that person.

Special Depreciation Allowance - Additional depreciation during the first year of ownership of an asset, IRC Section 168(k). Being phased out year by year.

Special Use Vehicle - See Qualified Nonpersonal Use Vehicle

Standard Mileage Rate - The IRS allows taxpayers to deduct driving expenses for certain activities on a per mile basis. The 2023 mileage rates for qualifying activities are 65.5 cents for business, 22 cents for medical , and 14 cents for charity.

Subcontractor - A worker who is treated as being self-employed, that takes care of their own taxes and has more control over their own work.

Tax Avoidance - Legal methods of reducing taxes.

Tax Evasion - Illegal scheme to willfully hide income and pay less tax.

Tax Incentive - The government subsidizes economic activity by giving business tax exclusions, exemptions, deductions and credits.

Tax Shelter - Investment, asset, or activity to reduce taxes.

Tax Year - A 12-month period upon which taxes will be assessed. See Fiscal Year; Calendar Year

Taxable Income - the income left over after subtracting allowable deductions and adjustments, upon which the tax liability will be computed.

Unearned Income - Income which is not worked for such as investments, dividends and interest. Unearned income of a child can trigger the Kiddie Tax.

Useful Life - The number of years an asset is expected to be economically viable before needing to be replaced, which generally equals the recovery period.

Vehicle Class - Car, heavy SUV, heavy truck, are determined by the GVWR with the other class being special use vehicle is determined by the likelihood of the vehicle being appropriate for personal use.

Works Cited

Law

26 USC - Internal Revenue Code (IRC)

IRS Publications

IRS Pub 15 - Employer's Tax Guide

IRS pub 15-A - Employer's Supplemental Tax Guide

IRS Pub 15-B - Employer's Tax Guide to Fringe Benefits

IRS Pub 334 - Tax Guide for Small Business

IRS Pub 463 - Travel - Gift - Car Expenses

IRS Pub 535 - Business Expenses

IRS Pub 541 - Partnerships

IRS Pub 542 - Corporations

IRS Pub 550 - Investment Income and Expenses

IRS Pub 583 - Starting a Business and Keeping Records

IRS Pub 587 - Business Use of Your Home

IRS Pub 946 - How to Depreciate Property

IRS Pub 3402 - Taxation of LLC

BOOKS BY THIS AUTHOR

Banking, Borrowing and Budgeting
Personal Finance for Students and Parents

<u>Honors and Awards</u>

"#2 Best Budgeting Books of 2022"
-BookAuthority.org

<u>Amazon Reviews</u>

"...incredibly helpful...."

"...concise and easy to understand."

"This is exactly what high schoolers and college students need."

"If you care about your child's financial future or even just need a better foundation for yourself, this book is a fabulous place to start."